Ways to Go

PLANES GO!

By John Matthew Williams

Gareth Stevens
PUBLISHING

Please visit our website, www.garethstevens.com. For a free color catalog of all our high-quality books, call toll free 1-800-542-2595 or fax 1-877-542-2596.

Cataloging-in-Publication Data

Names: Williams, John Matthew.
Title: Planes go! / John Matthew Williams.
Description: New York : Gareth Stevens Publishing, 2018. | Series: Ways to go | Includes index.
Identifiers: ISBN 9781538210208 (pbk.) | ISBN 9781538210239 (library bound) | ISBN 9781538210215 (6 pack)
Subjects: LCSH: Airplanes–Juvenile literature.
Classification: LCC TL547.W55 2018 | DDC 629.13–dc23

First Edition

Published in 2018 by
Gareth Stevens Publishing
111 East 14th Street, Suite 349
New York, NY 10003

Editor: Kate Mikoley
Designer: Sam DeMartin

Photo credits: Cover, p. 1 MO_SES Premium/Shutterstock.com; p. 5 Sonpichit Salangsing/Shutterstock.com; p. 7 Alexey Y. Petrov/Shutterstock.com; pp. 9, 24 (wing) SAHACHATZ/Shutterstock.com; pp. 11, 24 (airport) EQRoy/Shutterstock.com; p. 13 Rawpixel.com/Shutterstock.com; pp. 15, 24 (pilot) Angelo Giampiccolo/Shutterstock.com; p. 17 Mike Fuchslocher/Shutterstock.com; p. 19 Joseph M. Arseneau/Shutterstock.com; p. 21 stockphoto mania/Shutterstock.com; p. 23 Sergey Novikov/Shutterstock.com.

Printed in the United States of America

CPSIA compliance information: Batch #CW18GS: For further information contact Gareth Stevens, New York, New York at 1-800-542-2595.

Contents

Flying Fast 4

People on Planes. 12

Big and Small 16

Going All Over 20

Words to Know 24

Index. 24

Planes go fast!

They fly in the sky.

Planes have wings.
Wings help the plane go.

Planes leave from an airport.

American
HSBC

People who go on planes
are called passengers.

A pilot flies the plane.

Some planes are big.

VP-BNZ

Some are small.

ATP
ATP

Planes can fly
over the sea.

They go all over the world.

Words to Know

wing

airport

pilot

Index

airport 10
passengers 12
pilot 14
wings 8